Reflections From Upriver 2015

What the Media Didn't Tell You

12/31/2015

Brent Shapiro

For my parents, Tom and Kay Curtis who taught me that one person can make a difference.

****

Forward

The series of articles contained in this book can be found at Colkurtz.com. The focus of the articles is to give the readers insights considered too politically incorrect to be covered correctly (except in hindsight) by the mainstream media.

The articles are presented for your reading pleasure, by publishing date. Many were written as events occurred in real time. By writing in the moment, I had a few large misses (see the Trump article). However, I'd rather admit being wrong in the present and adjust to current realities, rather than be that poser (we all know at least one) claiming they had the answers all along. That is the reason why this book and its contents were copyrighted on 31 December 2015.

It is my hope that this series of articles will you allow a few moments of reflection on topics seen on a daily basis but presented in an apolitical perspective, and not bound to the altar of political correctness.

Many thanks, and please enjoy!

Brent Shapiro

Table of Contents

A Hero's Death

10 March 2015

The videotaped death of Jordanian Air Force pilot Lieutenant Muath al Kasasbeh was another attempt by ISIS to prove they are the most violent and vicious entity operating in the Greater Middle East. As a recruiting too,l this particular video may have limited success in garnering support. There are those who may be enamored with the thought of operating under the banner of "No Quarter."

However, this horrific video had an opposite effect as it showed Lt. Muath al Kasasbeh in quiet prayer before and during the moments his life ended in flames. Some say death is never noble but inevitable. In this instance I must disagree. This young man knew his death and its manner was imminent. He also knew his family would see and be judged by his courage and composure at death. In those horrible moments he gathered himself and met fate with dignity. By doing so his family's honor was enhanced and ISIS failed to capture what it wanted most, the death of a coward begging for mercy.

In conclusion, when ISIS fighters attempt to surrender or change sides during a battle or conflict (which is the tribal way), what, if any, courage and composure will they possess when they are shown "No Quarter"?

Putin's Gambit

15 March 2015

On 29 November 2014 OPEC nations (led by Saudi Arabia) met in Vienna and decided not to cut current oil production levels that would affect the price or reduce the glut of oil on the global market. This declaration has profound negative impacts on some principal players on the world stage and may contribute to their economic and political instability. Russia, Iran, and Venezuela are the first nations that come to mind. They are reliant, to the extreme, on the price of oil and are most distressed by this announcement.

Since Russia's armed annexation of the Crimea and the continued offensive operations in the eastern Ukrainian regions of Donesk and Luhansk, the receding price of oil and the devaluation of the Russian currency against the dollar have been nothing short of spectacular. Since June 1, 2014 the Ruble has fallen from .02865 to a record low of 0.1403 on December 16, a 49% decrease in purchasing power for the Russian government. The devaluation of the Ruble and the equally impressive drop in the price of oil from $95 bbl. to $55.15 is causing President Putin and Russian leader-ship/oligarchs to ponder Russia's current policies towards Ukraine and its western neighbors.

In 2012, economists in the Russian Federation stated that for it to meet its debt obligations oil needed to be priced at $120 bbl. (taking into consideration the current quarterly Ruble/USD exchange rate of 0.3408/1.00). Since the Ruble's devaluation against the dollar, the true value for the price of Russian oil needs to be valued at $177.50 in order to maintain its current balance of payments. Russia and other nations purchase energy and other commodity contracts that range in different lengths of time. However, most of the short-term contracts lasting up to 6 months are expiring. Values of future contracts for oil, natural gas, and other commodities that drive Russian drive the Russian economy to include gold, silver, and palladium will be valued in relation to spot world commodity market pricing.

When faced with the vast Russian currency devaluation against the dollar and lower commodity prices, the proabability of the Russian Federation being able to finance itself, meet international its debt obligations, or insure the Russian people have the ability to feed themselves or heat their home in the long term is a serious question that must be asked. Since the summer of 2014, the Russian economy has been sliding into recession. As a rule, economic recessions always look better and non-threatening on paper by those who only read of them. However, the non-academic reality and real time depression in many sectors of the Russian economy are not only affecting the average Russian people, but also the oligarchs who, are losing up to one billion dollars a day due to international sanctions.

The United States, the European Union and others started imposing crippling economic sanctions against Russia shortly after the military annexation of Crimea and the continued injection of Russian forces into the eastern regions of Donesk, Luhansk, Mariupol, and Khershon regions. Since that time, Russian President Putin has made headlines by stating Russia will start diversifying energy delivery by signing trade agreements to supply oil and natural gas to China and India and endeavoring to make the relationships lasting by building pipelines to terminals in those countries. Supplying the increasing South Asian demand for energy is a goal Russia must act upon in the long term. These pronouncements make for good press domestically, but in the near and mid-term might be considered a fool's errand considering the Russians will be negotiating from a drastically inferior position politically and economically.

Currently, the Russian Federation does not possess the financial resources to build or maintain thousands of miles of natural gas and oil pipelines stretching from its Central Region to terminals in China and India. The money and technical expertise required to build and maintain the infastructure presently do not exist due to the embargo of western technology, financing, and lack of skilled labor necessary to implement these projects. If China were to finance these infrastructure projects it would be to Russia's disadvantage.

There are many substantial obstacles for Chinese participation in these energy infrastructure projects. Some of those include:

1) Since Russia does not have the manpower qualified to build and maintain the logistical system, the Chinese may insist on using their own skilled/unskilled labor, facilitators, and contractors to build the systems.. Currently, the Chinese government uses these techniques in Africa and other areas in the third world. This will lead to continued unemployment of the local population and many Russians would not be eligible for many contracts that service Chinese projects. This has led to animosity among populations in other nations that at times escalate into violence in regions where these contracts are currently in place.

2) For the xenophobic Russian government, the thought of hundreds of thousands of Chinese colonizing Russia under the guise of developing and maintaining long term energy infrastructure projects can be nothing more than a ruse to threaten the West.

3) If the pipelines are built and maintained by some miracle, the cost of financing would most likely be borne by the governments of China and India. The multi-billion dollar projects and subsequent maintenance costs would severely limit Russian ability to dictate a reasonable price for energy production and delivery to terminals in Asia. In addition, Russia still would not be able to take advantage of bi-lateral currency exchange rates for the energy, as the Chinese peg the Yuan to the price of the dollar, and the Indian Rupee value is prone to radical manipulation by its own government. Therefore, the price paid for Russian energy by China and India would

not consistently meet the cost of production and delivery of energy to destinations.

4)   Presently, there are few options President Putin can make in the near term regarding the Crimea and the Donesk/Luhansk regions that will benefit the Russian people. If Putin can politically survive coming off his wartime/patriotic domestic persona with no advantage to the Russian people (that's a big if), there are a number of measures he or the next leader of the Russian Federation may undertake as a matter of statecraft to accomplish stated goals in the region, knowing the United States and the West will not shed their blood for the sake of Ukrainian territorial integrity.

a)   Continue to recognize Donesk and Luhansk as autonomous regions and defend them economically, politically, and in covert military manners that insure the current de facto political realities on the ground become stable, irreversible, and in time deemed legitimate.

b)   Guide those governments to maintain their semi-autonomous status within Ukraine in order to maintain internal instability and use that power to deter central government attempts to join NATO or the European Union.

c)   Tamp down the overt unrest in eastern Ukraine while continuing to use Russian Special Forces as cadre to stir racial and ethnic tensions in the Mariupol and Kershon regions. Use time as an ally, wait until western sanctions are lifted, and enter these regions under the guise of protecting Russian-speaking people, and secura a land bridge to the Crimea to ease the logistical hardships of supplying the Russian Black Sea Fleet.

The time factor, or Putin's lack of using time as his ally, has been the "crux of the biscuit" for those watching the situation develop between Russia and the Ukraine since the Spring of 2014. Russia, under Putin's leadership, could have taken the measures listed in the beginning. Using time as his advantage, he could have exerted and crafted measures (some would call it statesmanship) whereby he would have been able to accomplish their goals in the Crimea and eastern Ukraine. This could have been done without incurring the crippling sanctions currently imposed by the West and concurrent measures taken by Saudi Arabia to maintain their share of the world oil market that is bankrupting the Russian economy.

What lies ahead for the Russian people and its neighbors? Since Putin has waged war against Ukraine and a larger rhetorical war "against the liberal ideas of the United States and the West," what will happen when ordinary Russians tire of rhetoric and demand the lifting of sanctions? When will Russian oligarchs, the final arbiters of Russian power, tire of losing billions of dollars monthly and demand a change in leadership to effect the lifting of Western sanctions?

The most serious question regarding Russian internal politics is who will remove Putin from power and in what time frame? Will the removal come in the form of mass protests against Putin and his ministers similar to the demonstrations in 1917, or the Arab Spring of 2011? Or will the regime/oligarchs execute a coup d'état before the economy is again bankrupt and the Russian people finally demand a more transparent and open government complete with economic reforms.

After the question of Russian leadership is resolved, another equally important question remains. Will the next leader deescalate tensions and use time, western apathy, and political fatigue to accomplish its goals in eastern Ukraine? Or will Russian leadership continue to blackmail its neighbors by threatening to blockade contracted natural gas shipments, or will the new/old regime heighten military tensions that may lead to a new war, hot or cold, fought on an interconnected global battlefield.

"Listening In"

26 March 2015

The media in general and the talking bobbleheads on 24-hour news in particular have been bloviating at length regarding Israel's "Listening In" concerning negotiations about Iran's ongoing nuclear program. Newsflash! Israel's intelligence services gather intelligence on issues that it regards as threats to its national security. The United States makes few distinctions regarding the topic and has taken to surveiling everyone! This breaking news should have taken no one by surprise. For Israel to gather information regarding U.S./Iranian nuclear negotiations by any number of means (including simply speaking to members of the French nuclear delegation) is a matter of statecraft. However, sharing that information with members of the U.S. Congress behind Mr. Obama's back is impolite. Since Mr. Obama stated in a major foreign policy address in May 2011 that "Israel must be able to defend itself – by itself – against any threat," Israeli leadership felt compelled to make transparent to the public "The Deal" our vainglorious president planned to remain private and force it on the citizens of the United States as a matter of policy.

Mr. Obama views the threat of Iran possessing nuclear weapons as a threat to global commerce as opposed to a national security concern. Israel perceives Iranian possession of nuclear weapons as a existential threat that has merit, as the government of Iran has repeatedly declared the destruction of the State of Israel as a national priority since 1979.

Currently, Iran possesses a Medium Range Ballistic Missile System (MRBM) called the SHAHAB 3 that has the range to strike Israel. Those missiles, in time, will be mated with modified nuclear payloads. They also supply Hezbollah, Hamas, and Syria with weapons and expertise. Many in the Israeli government believe that it is only a matter of time when nuclear arms of some type will be included in future arms packages.

There are more than a few facts being avoided or ignored in coverage by the media.

1) Iran's possession of nuclear weapons is more of a menace to its Sunni Arab neighbors in the Gulf than anyone else. This fear is leading to an arms race that is only good for the suppliers of advanced weapons systems.

2) Iran will be able to blackmail its way out of sanctions completely by ensuring (threatening) the safe passage of oil through the Strait of Hormuz.

3) Iran will play a more prominent role in setting the price of oil on world markets as a member of OPEC by simply being the sole member of the cartel with nuclear weapons.

Other (similar) doomsday predictions were made when Russia and China became part of the Nuclear Club. Central Asia became a more interesting place when those loveable archenemies India and Pakistan announced their "Club" membership over the most militarized border on earth. Yet somehow, we have not only survived but thrived.

In conclusion, no regime of sanctions or number of military strikes will prevent Iran from obtaining nuclear weapons. In the past, any state with the capability and the will regardless of sanctions (see: North Korea) has built and successfully tested nuclear weapons.

We will have to do what we have done since the beginning of the Nuclear Age: that is not to wage war by any means on an intercontinental scale, but continue to fight our wars (if we must fight) by proxy and continue to have governments talk each other to death.

Arab Boots on Yemeni Soil

2 April 2015

Arab leaders of Gulf Cooperation Council (GCC), led by Saudi Arabia, have agreed to form a joint military force. It has taken these leaders four years of political and tribal warfare and escalating to the point of genocide before deciding to tacking action. If 2011 was the birth of the Arab Spring, 2015 can be seen as its demise. It is hard to believe that during last four years the leaders of the Gulf States have done nothing to mitigate the influences of ISIS in Iraq. Aside from the occasional airstrike to bolster domestic support Egypt has been smart by staying out of Libya, allowing the tribes to fight each other into exhaustion.

So why is the splitting of Yemen into two tribal entities who are deadly enemies worth such concern? Yes, the Sunni-based al-Qaeda in the Arabian Peninsula (AQAP) owns half of the country and the Shi'ite Houthi tribe that controls the other half is inconvenient, but they pose little physical threat to those outside their borders. Yemen is the bastard child of two failed states that merged in 1990, in accordance with western political tradition. This current division reflects Yemen's historical and natural tribal boundaries.

If there is any question about what is to be done in the region by local actors, I have a few suggestions:

    1) Create an air-to-ground task force drawn from Gulf Cooperation Council air forces to eliminate most offensive weapons of both AQAP and the Houthi tribal militas. This would leave mainly light/defensive weapons to maintain the current tribal and religious status quo. Light arms in the hands of

tribesmen has never been, and will never be, a problem so long as they aim them in each others general direction.

2) Use the GCC air force to diminish and isolate ISIS forces that threaten Syria/Iraqi Kurdistan and the kingdom of Jordan until a political/tribal settlement can be reached between the tribes that support ISIS and all others.

3) Do not attempt to create a mirrored ground force. For decades getting NATO countries to put troops under a foreign commander was difficult, and at times not possible. Putting Arab troops under the command of anyone other than a local commander is a fool's errand and any foreign troops on the ground (Arab or otherwise) will be considered an invader by all warring Yemeni factions.

The crisis in Yemen is nothing more than a tribal/family feud. Local tribal leaders will put aside differences and fight together any they do not know. Therefore, allow the tribes in Iraq, Syria and Yemen to fight amongst themselves until they are exhausted or annihilated. Let them come to their own conclusions regarding when and how to negotiate peace. If a solution not made by their own council, the peace will be resented and undermined. A dictated peace in this case will just be hitting the reset button on the events that led to this mess and lead to a protracted war involving all neighbors in the region.

All the World's a Stage

5 April 2015

"All the world is indeed a stage and we are merely players, performers and portrayers, each another's audience outside the gilded cage."
- Neil Peart

In Lausanne, Switzerland, the United States and Iran are engaging in global theater. Facts on the ground in Iran are outrunning political considerations. It is inevitable that Iran will possess nuclear weapons capability within the next decade. Against this backdrop the United States is laying the groundwork whereby the largest sponsor of state terrorism will magically transform into a responsible member of the Nuclear Weapons Club. The phased lifting of sanctions in return for inspections of nuclear facilities is the supposed carrot for the Iranian regime. However, that carrot is a red herring for foreign consumption as no sanctions or military actions will deter Iran from obtaining nuclear weapons.

The Obama Administration believes the world must be desensitized to the thought of a nuclear Iran. In this, President Obama is correct. The world does need time to digest that Iran will be a member of the Nuclear Weapons Club. The Obama Administration, by using the world as a stage is crafting a climate whereby nations in the Arabian Gulf, given time, may plan to peacefully (or not) deal with this evolving development.

This fait accompli "Deal" with the Iranian regime is a bitter pill to swallow in light of its current involvement in Iraq, Syria, Yemen, and its role in sponsoring terror abroad. Over time, the areas in direct conflict will diminish as the people of these

Drone On!

7 May 2015

Over the last six years, the Obama administration has dramatically increased the number of drone strikes in the Afghanistan/Pakistan region during our war on Islamic terrorists. It has recently been revealed that the losses have been so devastating in these regions that the senior ranks of Al Qaeda's leadership have lost their pre-eminence to the more violent junior affiliates located in Yemen and Somalia. Now that two American hostages have been killed by accident, the twenty-four-hour news and mainstream media bobbleheads' national debate "drones on" regarding the tactical use of drones as part of a global anti-terror strategy worthy of emulation and continuation.

The media has made the inadvertent death of Americans killed by a drone strike (that also killed two senior Al Qaeda leaders) nothing more than a means of selling daily programming. The media and like-minded individuals have little idea, or worse, do not care, that implementing a Drone Czar will only add a time-consuming layer of bureaucracy to the time sensitive nature of the vast majority of terror/counter-terror missions. If the argument is carried further, and requires a guarantee of absolutely no civilian casualties, the drone and all other kinetic programs and the lives they have saved over the last twelve years will be shelved due to political (not military) ineptitude. Jihadists will then be emboldened, and will rearm and train safely behind the skirts of their women and children. This recipe has been written and refined by Hezbollah in Southern Lebanon and Hamas in Gaza over the last twenty-five years.

Currently, the U.S. has three options regarding how to deal with global terrorism:

1) We can put boots on the ground in every terror haven until the end of time and still not succeed in eliminating threats.

2) We can continue to launch air strikes that will only increase civilian suffering and collateral damage without eliminating terrorism and possibly have the world view terrorists as victims.

3) There is the unthinkable option of discontinuing all military action and allow terrorist organizations and their affiliates to pursue their agendas without interference.

Or, we can continue to utilize the drone program as part of a multi-layered approach to fight and confine terrorism, reduce collateral damage, and limit civilian casualties despite these criminals' insistence on operating and living openly with their families in built-up urban areas.

"Not on My Block"

11 May 2015

Over the last four years, the sheer number of Africans that have made the perilous journey to Southern Europe by boat has been staggering. This continued migration makes the Cuban Mariel Boat lift of 1980 look like a Boy Scout troop crossing an intermittent stream in New Mexico in August. Since the ill-timed removal of Libyan ruler, Muammar Gaddafi from power in 2011, Sub-Saharan Africans have flocked to Libyan ports with the intent of crossing the Mediterranean Sea by any means to find sanctuary on the shores of Europe.

In the weeks of 14-28 April 2015, over 13,000 immigrants have been rescued by the Italian Navy and merchant vessels, and at least 1,000 have died in the attempt. To date, nearly 120,000 immigrants have reached European shores, with approximately another one million ready to make the attempt.

A major contributing factor in this catastrophe is the unintended consequence brought on primarily by Western countries over the last thirty plus years. What was intended to be a noble gift for the people of Africa by providing childhood vaccinations, health care, and the ability of the world to feed these people, has over the decades, become something less. As a result, many parts of Africa are vastly overpopulated with more than 40% of the total population under the age of 19. Nature's methods of regulating and balancing the population has been thwarted for the most part by these "good deeds" which now plays a major in the humanitarian crisis that is spreading beyond the shores of the African continent.

This population explosion, accompanied by western Equatorial Africa's inability to harness and equitably distribute its vast natural resources in order to provide basic services to the population, add to the suffering of millions on the continent. This man-made humanitarian crisis not only impacts the lives of present and future migrants, but has prompted moral, political, and ethical debates throught Europe regarding how to manage, integrate, and assimilate those who come ashore.

On May 10, the EU Foreign Affairs Policy Office announced the first policies regarding African refugees. However, many European leaders will find it politically difficult to implement these policies or future directives due to current racial, ethnic, and social unrest unique to each nation.

Bring Back Good Management

1 June 2015

By and large, companies and institutions of all sizes use time-tested practices and behave in certain manners meant to keep them in business. This does not mean those businesses have the best products or services, but it suggests that they may have certain advantages others do not. A myriad of factors including, liquidity, location, scale, purchasing power, and the ability to drive competitors out of an area by operating at a loss, are but a few techniques used to ensure a company's ability to do business in any economic climate.

In many instances, businesses/institutions that in the past have been leaders and pioneers in their fields either introduced innovative products or provided outstanding services. Some classic examples include Eastman Kodak, Pan American Airlines, AOL (America Online), and the N.W.A. These pioneers and innovators provided good management and for decades were deemed the gold standard in their respective fields. However, all went bankrupt or were integrated into companies that had a better understanding of "What Was to Come Next."

Not all companies/institutions are doomed to fail, but many adhere to several of the same practices. However, over the years, one practice in particular has spread to pandemic proportions across many spectrums to include business, academia, and all levels of government. That practice is known as *"leadership by, and for, the average."* In the defense of their "particular brand," many institutions use "The Company Way" to ingrain practices and modes of thinking at all levels of management in order to maintain their personal legacy. Many of these silent, unofficial policies abhor deviations from standard (and often ethical) practices, regardless of benefits to the institution, and **terminate with extreme prejudice** those who utilize unauthorized methods and talents in the name of defending a particluar institutions brand.

To illustrate this point, many institutions over the years have allowed and encouraged the blurring of the lines that separate management and talent/staff. In the past it was not so. Management was directed to ensure their staff was adequately trained and that time, resources, and talents of their team were coordinated to consistently accomplish goals and directives. However, since the early 1990's, institutions have been hiring management at all levels who involve themselves in processes and applications they are not suited for. By insisting on operating in this co-mingled role of management/talent, they become neither, and the results in many cases, are less than what should be expected. These individuals, instead, lose sight of long-term goals and as a result, lose the ability to manage their staff, waste valuable time, and neglect specialized assets required for task completion.

A main rationale for the behavior of this new breed of micro-managers is that many believe their jobs may be in jeopardy when staff members are more knowledgeable in certain specialized areas.

What they fail to realize, and what higher management fails to instill in new management hires, *is their job is to manage time, resources, and staff talent. It is not management's job to compete with the talented staff or directly involve themselves in duties below their pay grade. (For instance, a commander in the army complained how I ran my unit even though it was one of the more highly rated units in the division. I respectfully told that commander I would gladly command his brigade for six months if he chose to exchange pay and command responsibilities.)*

I realize there is a tendency to inject personal preferences in all aspects of of their environment, it is human nature. However, upper management across all spectrums must explain to lower level managers that job evaluations will be graded only on how well they ***manage their staff and resources*** in relation to tasks that must completed successfully, and on a consistent basis. By enforcing this credo, management will no longer be intimidated by others' expertise and will cease to take personal credit and plagiarize work of others since these accomplishments will no longer be part of job performance evaluations for retention or promotion.

In conclusion, institutions must instill in new management hires at all levels that their performance will be rated only on management skills and job completion. By getting rid of these faux managers, it is hoped the blurred lines created by the hiring of those who inappropriately take personal and professional credit for the work of their talented staffs will be overcome. The next generation of management will then be called upon to use their abilities to foster talents, expertise, creativity and teamwork. In this manner, managers will be safe in the knowledge their jobs and promotions are dependent on how well they operate as leaders, managers, and organizers. In return, the American people will benefit by having our government, companies, and institutions function more efficiently and will be able to respond more effectively to a variety of different economic, political, military, and social environments.

A Day of Bipartisanship

15 June 2015

On Tuesday, June 9th, the 114th Congressional session came together in a bipartisan manner and derailed President Obama's attempt to gain autocratic trade negotiating powers by soundly defeating the workers' aid program that was a keystone segment of the agreement making up the Trans-Pacific Partnership (TPP). The TPP includes 11 Asia Pacific countries including, Australia, Brunei Darussalam, Canada, Chile, Japan, Malaysia, Mexico, New Zealand, Peru, Singapore, and Vietnam. If given the vote, the Obama Administration would have the authority to negotiate terms of this very important trade agreement without the input of Congress. Congress would be limited to either passing the legislation or not. The use of "fast track authority," or trade promotion authority (TPA), was originally used from 1975 to 1994 under the Trade Act of 1974 and again from 2002 to 2007 under the Trade Act of 2002, and is a temporary power granted to the President by Congress to negotiate international agreements. Although a temporary power, it is controversial in that Congress can approve or disapprove the agreement, but cannot amend or filibuster once authorized. Fifteen of twenty trade agreements have been passed using "fast track authority." On June 9, the Bipartisan Congressional Trade Priorities Act of 2014, meant to give President Obama "fast track authority" to finalize upcoming trade negotiations with Asia-Pacific countries and Europe, was blocked by Congress.

It would be very polite to say our elected officials cast their votes as a matter of principal, but this is simply not the case. Since the mid-1970s, many American industries have been forced to close due to unfair trade practices of countries like China and Japan who use their ability to manipulate their currencies and allow companies to form consortiums to force competing manufactures and companies out of business. For instance, how many reading here remember televisions or radios made in America? Our country has laws governing anti-dumping and currency manipulation, but Presidents over the last forty years have chosen not to enforce most violations by various trading partners.

Between the lax enforcement of U.S. laws and the rise of free trade agreements (13 since the inception of the North American Free Trade Agreement), over one million jobs have been lost in manufacturing industries, including steel and automotive, which have since been forced to close or consolidate operations. Moreover, the U.S. trade deficit with NAFTA partners Mexico and Canada is an estimated $181 billion. Nationally, with the erosion of the manufacturing sector, there are fewer jobs that pay a living wage that do not require adding to personal debt. At the local level, this loss means there is less of a tax base to fund schools and basic infrastructure projects, thereby forcing municipalities to raise sales and property taxes to balance their budget.

In 2009, the Obama Administration could have taken steps by executive action that would have revived the economy and put Americans back to work. By executive order (Obama loves to use this), the president could have mandated that only products made in America be used in the shovel-ready infrastructure projects, and only automobiles made by U.S. companies be eligible for tax incentives for the Cash-for-Clunkers program. Instead, cheap and many times substandard steel from India, China, and Japan were dumped on U.S. markets for use in many of these projects. Consequently, the long term winners in both of these programs were grateful foreign automobile and manufacturing companies who employed their citizens, avoided U.S. taxes, and sent the U.S. stimulus money straight home.

The key to acceptable future trade agreements is to make them reciprocal in most ways that benefit each trading partner. For instance, many countries, especially those in Asia, do not allow many American-made products into their country. To add insult to injury, many of these countries do not allow foreign ownership of businesses on their soil and force those companies doing business in their country to partner with local entities. This issue has led to decades long grievances with China, in particular, regarding the piracy of intellectual property of junior business partners.

In conclusion, I understand the role that trade (free or not) has played in stabilizing Europe and many countries in the Pacific region since the end of World War II. However, the continued preferential treatment of imported goods and services at the expense of products made here in America must end.

A Double Standard

30 June 2015

On Monday, June 22 2015, the United Nations Commission on Human Rights (UNCHR) announced that a U.N. investigative panel found credible evidence that Israel and militant Palestinian groups committed war crimes during the 2014 conflict in Gaza.

A casual reader might interpret the article as fairly balanced but on closer inspection, it is another in a long series of revisionist historical (some say hysterical) narratives that attempt to negate Israel's legitimate right to exist and protect its citizens.

To be fair, the Independent Inquiry of the 2014 Gaza Conflict did report "the primary purpose of Palestinian rocket attacks was to spread terror in the civilian population." It also stated that over six thousand missiles and mortars were launched into Israel, and in return Israel responded in kind with a similar number of projectiles via counter-battery fire and airstrikes. However, the report lamented the disparity of civilian casualties suffered by the citizens of Gaza (1,462) as opposed to (6) Israeli civilians and the massive destruction of Palestinian infrastructure that left more than 100,000 Gazan's homeless.

What the report left out is that since 2001 there have been more than 18,000 rockets and mortars fired from within the Gaza Strip against civilian targets in Israel. There is continuing outrage and condemnation for Israel responding to these persistent attacks on its citizens but no condemnation for politicans and local leaders who use their civilian population centers, schools, and places of worship as safe havens for terrorists and missle batteries.

It is not hard to imagine what would happen if Mexico sent mortar rounds flying into border towns in south Texas or if the citizens of Calais launched a single missile toward the cliffs of Dover. There would be very little in the way of polite discussion or outrage regarding actions the United States and Great Britain would take to safeguard its citizens and discourage similar aggression.

Hamas leadership insists on causing the death and suffering of their own people, the destruction of their infrastructure, and places of worship in order to further their political agenda. Since these facts are not in question, I have one of my own. What is restraining the International Criminal Court (ICC) from proclaiming "Palestinian Lives Matter," issuing arrest warrants, and prosecuting those responsible for the deaths of their fellow Palestinians?

The U.S. Under Attack

8 July 2015

Many have pondered what a coordinated cyber attack might look like. This morning we might have glimpsed (in a very minor way since there are no body bags yet) what may come.

On 8 July between 8:00 and 9:45 a.m. ET United Airlines (UAL) cancelled 76 flights and delayed 1,400 others due to a malfunctioning computer router. Between 11:32 a.m. and 3:10 p.m. ET, trading on the New York Stock Exchange (NYSE) was halted for what has been called "Internal Technical Issues". During this time, servers in China have mounted a sustained and massive attack on a company headquartered in St. Louis, MO. By monitoring the number of sustained Chinese attacks on the city of St. Louis and tertiary/follow-on attacks on Seattle, WA and Long Beach, CA, it leads me to believe that Boeing, the worlds largest aerospace/defense company, as the specific target. For those who want to see this attack in real time go to http://map.norsecorp.com/

The FBI and the Department of Homeland Security have tentatively ruled out criminal action (yea, right) at the NYSE and UAL. Those conclusions are not based on facts, as the investigations are in the preliminary stage. However, the probability of these huge technological problems happening on the same day and approximately the same time a sustained and coordinated cyber attack on one of America's most respected companies is too coincidental. If you take into consideration the Chinese stock markets are off by as much as 40% and may be in the first stages of a financial crisis (similar to our 2008 banking disaster) that might have significant political consequences and you might have a adversary who needs to send a message (perhaps with the help of other like minded friends) to the world to "back off" or have certain industries, electrical grids, or even nursing homes become unwanted centers of attention.

Or How I loved the Persian Bomb

21 July 2015

I don't love "The Iranian Bomb" or any other weapon of mass destruction used to terrorize others. However, no amount of political or economic pressure has deterred any country from developing and testing nuclear weapons. For instance, the only thing North Korea had to do was to keep talking and beg for food and fuel for ten years, at which time they announced their membership in the "Nuclear Club."

Iran is just a bit different. They live in an area torn by civil, ethnic, religious, and tribal strife. They are a nation that actively supports, trains, and arms the Assad regime in Syria, Hezbollah in Lebanon, and Hamas in Gaza. By being the most hated and feared nation in the Middle East (yes, more than Israel) this situation is causing the most difficult dilemmas regarding the proliferation of nuclear weapons since 1949.

Iran possessing nuclear weapons is not a question of "if" but rather when. The way the "Deal" reads is this: there will be snap inspections (that is, if you consider military installations off limits) and inspections must be approved by Iranian authorities well in advance. But let's not get caught up in "The Deal", as Iran will probably use the North Korean model to ultimately render inspections as useful as using sandpaper for bathroom tissue.

The simple facts is that Russia, China, and a host of countries will begin trading with Iran regardless of ratification of this agreement by the U.S. Senate. U.S. sanctions will be a matter of little consequence compared to the trade, technology, and billions of dollars of frozen assets heading Iran's way in the near future. It is very possible Iranian leadership hopes the U.S. will not ratify this agreement. In this scenario Iran will have everything they want within one year: nuclear weapons capability and the ability to trade at will with China, Russia, (and a host of other nations) which will completely negate all repercussions from U.S. sanctions.

In conclusion, we can only hope the U.S. Senate ratifies this agreement and Iran slow plays their nuclear development hand similar to North Korea and allow other countries in the region the time to accept the eventual reality of the "Persian Bomb."

Do Black Lives Matter?

9 September 2015

Since growing up in East St. Louis, Illinois (my family left in 1975) I have heard my black friends bemoan how they are mistreated in every way, shape, and form by "The Man" (anyone who is not black). Being a Jewish kid who attended East St. Louis public schools from 1968-1975 gives me a different perspective on racial issues than what you hear from the mainstream media. Believe me, it was no picnic being in school when Martin Luther King and Robert Kennedy were assassinated.

Things were so bad that my grade school had to install bullet proof glass and chained/locked the school doors to protect the 6 white children from being assassinated by adults armed with guns or knives. Then, there was the gratuitous weekly bomb threats. During those times all students were corralled into the school cafeteria/gym where we line dance to the 5th Dimension's "Age of Aquarius/Let the Sunshine In" for hours.

To emphasize the insanity of the times, my very first hour of my first day in class was spent standing along the wall with my classmates waiting to be pulled over the lap of Miss Tate and beaten with a rubber paddle. To be fair, Miss Tate called my father and told him that she beat us all with a rubber paddle because we (the class) needed to fear her to maintain order and prevent violence (other than her paddle) from occurring in her class.

While my early years attending East St. Louis public schools were not pleasant I observed greater racial discrimination taking place within the black community itself. Bi-racial and light-skinned children had to endure more, for they were not considered black or white, but "House Negroes." However, the most violent of acts and humiliation were directed against black albino children and their families. All were looked upon as freaks and heretics by the black community (and we all know what happens to heretics), so it should surprise no one when I say they were long gone after first grade.

So when I hear "Black Lives Matter", I get very, very, angry. First, I believe "All Lives Matter," second I want to know where all the black outrage is regarding the overwhelming violence they inflict on their own communities each and every day. Many cannot flee the persistent neighborhood poverty and violence and live as prisoners in their homes as soon as the sun sets. Others fear for their children's lives each time they step out of their homes. Many individuals,especially children, are compelled to commit acts of violence in order to be accepted by their peers or out of fear they will be viewed as prey. This physical, psychological, social, and economic violence inflicted on black Americans by members of their own community fuels this cycle of violence, and poverty. In many communities these actions have been considered normal for many decades. Generations of black children (now adults) are being raised in this environment and learn from a young age to adapt and survive lest they become what they fear becoming most, perennial victims.

Yes, black lives do matter. However, black families must first tire of the perpetual violence committed in their neighborhood by members of their own community. Second, families must teach their children (if they cannot, then provide role models) how to support each other and live in peace and prosperity as a community. Third, they must deny any and all sanctuary and support, by any means, to those who prey upon their community. Fourth, if there are issues with local law enforcement (and there are), local/grass roots social services such as churches and other community centers should be used as bases for self-policing of neighborhoods, thus limiting the need for a heavy law enforcement presence.

It has taken decades for members of the black community to chant the mantra "Black Lives Matter." It is now up to the black communities to decide if they have the desire and long-term commitment to make better lives for their children/grand-children by ***owning the problems in their neighborhoods*** and utilize all measures to take back their streets. Only at that time will I agree "Black Lives Matter" as much to the black community.

If black communities cannot take back their streets they might decide not to burn their own homes and businesses as they did in Ferguson. They may instead decide to march on areas where county offices are located. This not so novel but seldom used approach will cause governments at the local, state, and federal level to react with greater force and violence against protestors. If wealthy white businesses are in danger, then a much larger national debate will occur.

Turn Out The Lights, The Party's Over

16 September 2015

The fantasy and good fun was refreshing while it lasted. However, the man who finally dashed two decades of political correctness on the national stage and set a course for a wider range of formerly untouchable conversations for all presidential pretenders must eventually meet reality.

During this evening's CNN Republican debate, Donald Trump will (I hope) finally be asked about his views regarding abortion and a women's right to choose. At that moment the fantasy of a Trump presidency will soon become nothing but a fond memory. Most important is what happens next. The "What's Next" will become required viewing for those who need a visual on how not to handle a crisis.

My question for the media is how long will they continue to cover a man who will be politically irrelevant and can only be nothing more than a parody of himself?

Please come back tomorrow and see if CNN had the guts to ask the Donald the question and if I called the fallout correctly. If the CNN moderators decline to ask presidential pretenders about their views on a women's reproductive rights (abortion) the suspense will continue to build.

Run Joe, Run!

21 September 2015

Joe, America shared your grief on the loss of your son Bo with you last week on The Late Show. Nothing compares with the grief of a parent over the loss of a child. However, the time of public grief is coming to an end, and it is time to come to the rescue of the Democratic Party. The political correctness forced on us during the Clinton Administration in the 90's is hopefully ending and America needs/wants a president who is transparent and genuine. For all the fun we have had at your expense you have proven to be both.

Being Mr. Irrelevant (Vice President) for the last 7 years in this political environment is a very good thing. Being recognized as a good man with a very shallow political footprint is a trait that all other presidential pretenders can only envy.

Joe, we need you to be the oldest first term elected president. For the sake of the American people, announce former ambassador Bill Richardson as your Vice President, surround yourself with the most forward looking and capable staff/cabinet to round out your administration and become the Ronald Regan of our generation

Joe, have the vision to guide this nation, utilize the talents/expertise of a professional apolitical staff, and wisely chart a new course for this nation and leave the memories of previous administrations of this millennia as a warning ...

Duck, and Cover!

8 October 2015

For more than a year the Russian Air Force has been conducting supply operations in the areas surrounding the Russian naval base in Lattakia, Syria. During the past month Russian air operations have expanded to include conducting ground attack missions on behalf of the Assad regime.

Recently, Russian ground forces have been on the move with armored infantry units and supporting organic heavy artillery batteries to combat zones and operating alongside and in conjunction with Syrian ground forces. This marks the first time since World War II that Russian forces have openly taken the field in the Middle East.

To further complicate matters, Russian aircraft have intercepted U.S. drones operating in Syrian airspace. This confluence of U.S., Turkish, and Russian forces operating in the same battlespace and using the same equipment as their Syrian allies greatly increases the odds of what I call "Kind of Friendly Fire" casualties. If/when soldiers on either side are reported dead/wounded, leaders in Russia, Turkey, and the U.S. may not have the luxury of being "Rational Actors". They may be driven by the pressures of public opinion, driven by 24hr news (they will be salivating for this) and social media to take military actions, to avenge in kind, in the name of national honor.

This "Balkanization" of Syria may very well introduce to this generation something it has never known (duck and cover), or feared: War with Russia.

For those that that have inquisitive minds, Ezekiel chapters 38 and 39 located in the Old Testament may provide interesting reading.

A Timely Intervention

8 November 2015

It has been reported the U.S. and other international powers (to include Russia) have resumed U.N. sponsored peace talks on Syria, and for the first time recognize that Assad will remain in power in the areas he controls for the foreseeable future. Well, la-de-da. Bashar al-Assad is the legitimate and internationally recognized leader of Syria (much to Mssr. Obama's chagrin) and has requested direct Russian military and economic aid. This marks the first time since 1946 that Russian ground forces have operate openly and at the behest of legitimate government in the Middle East.

Direct Russian military and economic intervention has stabilized Syria's Western Alawite Corridor which is becoming part of a larger political picture in Mesopotamia. This political picture is coalescing and solidifying into a Western Syria/Alawite Corridor, a semi contiguous Kurdish North Syria/Iraq, a truncated Shiah Iraq extending up to Anbar province, and a large Sunni Middle (Sunni Land for a lack of a better term) occupying vast amounts of territory that make up what we label Iraq and Syria.

Again, it must be clearly stated that direct Russian military intervention and resupply of the Assad regime has become the de facto stabilizing force in western Syria and is responsible for preventing the wholesale slaughter of over two million Alawite's (or in ISIS's eyes, heretics good for nothing more than death and slavery). As a byproduct, Russian intervention has prevented ISIS, operating as the military arm of the Sunni tribes, from becoming directly involved in the simmering sectarian violence in Lebanon where one of every three inhabitants are refugees. Russian forces are acting as a buffer another terrorist group uses recent migrants from North Africa/Middle East in these assaults, there may be disastrous consequences for those seeking asylum in Europe. If the people of Europe fear attacks from those who seek asylum, it may be politically impossible for their leaders to accept and incorporate these refugees/migrants into their society. If today's attacks had taken place in Hungary, Bulgaria, Croatia, or Greece, it is very possible these nations would have forcibly relocated these populations, militarily sealed their southern borders and returned those in the midst of crossing Mediterranean to other ports for debarkation.

For Turkey, this would be the ultimate nightmare. For the last five years, a national cottage industry has evolved, offering goods and services to migrants passing through on their way to European destinations. If the European land border is closed, Turkey will have to deal with the political and economic backwash of hundreds of thousands of migrant's trapped attempting to transit their country and the ever-growing number sitting on their border. At that time the migrant superhighway will become something else.